In the Pastor's Study

In the Pastor's Study

A Spiritual Journey into Self-Awareness

Abby Bates

Grateful Steps
Asheville, North Carolina

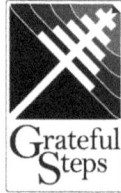

Grateful Steps Foundation
Crest Mountain
30 Ben Lippen School Road #107
Asheville, North Carolina 28806

Bates, Abby
In the Pastor's Study:
A Spiritual Journey into Self-Awareness
Illustrations by Becky LedBetter
Front and back cover photographs
by Nancy B. Webster are of
William Spencer Boyd Memorial Chapel
at Asheville School

ISBN 978-1-945714-30-6 Paperback
Printed in the United States of America
at Lightning Source

FIRST EDITION

www.gratefulsteps.org

I dedicate *In the Pastor's Study*
to Reverend Anne Morgan
and the late Reverend David Morgan,
both of whose faith and guidance helped
reawaken my spirituality.
In addition, I dedicate this volume to
Reverend Dent C. Davis III,
who was the first minister to
help me tap into my spirituality in a
deep and meaningful way!

CONTENTS

AUTHOR'S NOTE

I was born approximately two and a half weeks early on October 12, 1955, to older parents in Asheville, North Carolina. My mom was 35 and my dad was 44. Being older parents — with Dr. Spock as the only resource in those days — my parents did not know how to handle me. When I started school, the teachers quickly discovered that I had learning problems, as well as social and emotional difficulties. I was referred to both a neurologist and a psychologist who, after testing, diagnosed me with minimal brain damage, most likely due to circumstances surrounding my birth and early developmental days. I was a low-birthweight baby (5 lbs.), born about two and a half weeks early and delivered with the aid of forceps. In addition, at some point during my first year, I ran a high fever in conjunction with an ear infection.

In junior high, and as I transitioned into high school, I felt my parents didn't understand me and were against me; therefore, I was always on the defensive with them. My high school teachers encouraged me to express myself through poetry. Due to my learning difficulties and struggles with my parents, I wasn't a top-notch student. The administration at the private school I attended recommended that I transfer to public school, hoping that I would not feel the pressure to succeed. So, I transferred in the middle of my tenth grade year from private to public school.

Along with this transition to public school, I began seeing a psychiatrist. The psychiatrist and I, for the most part, just sat and stared at one another because I did not know how to put my thoughts and feelings into spoken words.

In 1978 a new minister, Reverend Dent C. Davis III, became the pastor at the church I grew up in — Oak Forest Presbyterian.

I connected with him immediately, very deeply at all levels, and he became my counselor. In the three and a half years that he counseled me, he helped me greatly to put feelings and words together, and I wrote many new poems. I had been "awakened" spiritually and emotionally.

Reverend Davis moved to Tennessee in 1981. Over the next eighteen years, I saw four different counselors.

Finally in 1998, I met the Reverends Anne and David Morgan and moved my church membership to New Hope Presbyterian Church. I knew I had come "full circle"—back to some real help. David became my counselor for the next twelve years.

In 2010, I felt as if I had reached a place of stability and was able to "let go" of the counseling relationship I had with David.

My poetry along with counseling has been my "saving grace" through the years. I've been able to dispel anger and many other confusing—for me—feelings.

Asking for and receiving counseling is a sign of strength and courage and has helped me overcome and work through my weaknesses, feelings and fears.

Publishing a book of my poetry has been a lifelong dream, and it brings me great joy that it is finally, at age 64, becoming a reality. I am so grateful that I connected with Grateful Steps Publishing, without which I would not have a book. To God be the glory!

Abby Bates

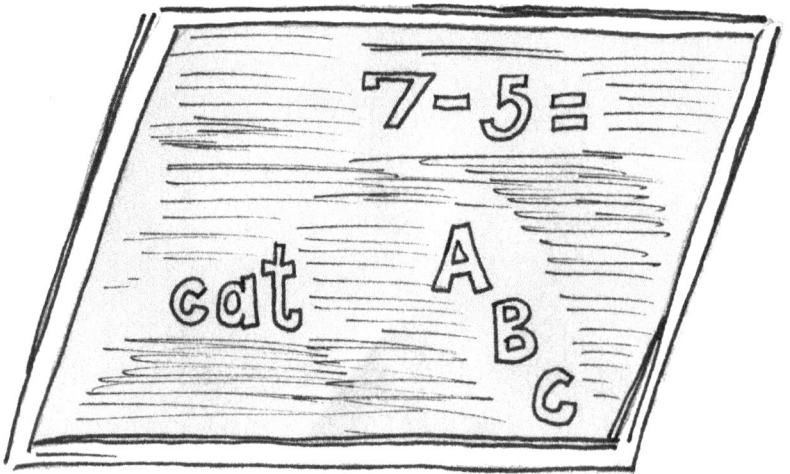

SCHOOL

RUNNING

I ran here, for no one loves me.
I sit and dream of the sky and sea.
I was treated like dirt.
Now I'm hurt.
I'm so lonely.
I sit and think of my life slowly.
I have nothing to live for.

1972–1973,
11th Grade

BUTTERFLIES

Butterflies are free
I wish I could be
Please someone set me free
Why do I feel this way?

I have so much to get out of life
And so much to give to others.

December 1972,
11th Grade

THE SUN

Fiery red, fiery yellow, fiery orange — The Sun.
If the sun dosen't rise
Nor shall I.
When the sun comes up
So will I.
The sun is bright.
It's put light into many lives.

1972–1973,
11th Grade

THE WIND

When the wind blows in the trees
You can see
The green leaves.

When the wind blows on the sea
The waves flow
Back to me.

1970–1971,
9th Grade

LIFE

Life is to be lived.
Life is real.
Life is to be enjoyed.
Not just a day
But everyday,
As long as you may live.

You may just sit your life away
Or You may love your life away.
Do what you may;
It's your life.

December 1972,
11th Grade

Holidays

SEASONS

GOODBYE TO SUMMER

The summer sun takes its exit slowly
Then forward into time we go
With fall's golden leaves
And winter's icy snow.
Onward. Onward to April's spring showers
And May's yellow flowers.
We've grown older,
Though summer's young again.

August 1972

EASTER IS

Easter is experiencing
the risen Christ in one's life
       and
springtime in the heart.

Easter is humans being set free
       and
triumphing o'er the bondage of
depression, fear and anxiety.

Easter is experiencing
new life through
Faith, Hope
       and
Love!

April 7, 1981

RENEWAL

Springtime brings the promise of renewed life!
Buds on trees ready to burst forth with green,
Flowers — daffodils, tulips and iris about to bloom,
Birds returning from their winter journey south;
Robin eggs in a nest
April showers bringing May flowers
Warm sunny days — shorts and short-sleeve weather
Activity all around
        and
Easter – celebrating the risen Christ!
The promise of hope, the promise of new life – springtime!

April 4, 1999

SUMMERTIME

Wildflowers and dandelions amidst fields of green—
An invitation to run and romp,
Neatly mowed yards—a lush green carpet of soft grass—
Inviting me to go barefoot.
A bright blue sky with fluffy white clouds—
Inviting me to lie on my back staring upward,
letting all my cares float away.
A centuries old oak tree, with branches
swaying gently in the breeze—
Inviting me to sit in the shade, sipping on lemonade,
on a hot summer day.
Summertime—and the Living is laid back!

April 2, 2002

CHRISTMAS IS

Christmas is snow on a winter day.
Christmas is children bright and gay.

Christmas is candy canes delicious and bright.
Christmas is many colorful lights.

Christmas is packages under the tree.
Christmas is a parade to see.

Christmas is Santa in his sleigh.
Christmas is Rudolph leading the way.

Christmas is a midnight mass.
Christmas is morning at last.

   But most of all,

Christmas is loving one and all.
Christmas is here at last.

December 1975

SUMMER INTO FALL

Green leaves turn to
Bright yellows, oranges, reds and browns;
There's a nip and chill
In the air!

Pumpkins are harvested,
Soon becoming jack-o-lanterns
On porches along the street.

The crunch of leaves is heard underfoot.
Darkness falls earlier,
Reminding us the days are growing shorter.

The smell of smoke is in the air
As fires in fireplaces are being built,

    Reminding us that

The winter solstice is near.

October 14, 2007

WELCOME SUMMER

Kick off your shoes—
Take a walk upon a carpet of soft, green grass
To the hammock for an afternoon nap.

Sip on ice coffee and ice tea.
Take a leisurely stroll,
Stopping along the way for a neighborly chat.

Hop on the tire swing—
Swing high up to the sky.
Head to the local swim hole.
Dive into the cool, fresh watrr to beat the afternoon heat.

Playing kids' games—"Mother, May I?" "Kick the can,"
Running to and fro
Catching fireflies,
Making lightning-bug lanterns.

Spread the blanket on the ground.
Bring out the chicken, lemonade and corn.
Crank the ice-cream freezer.
Everybody gather round—time for a picnic.
Welcome summertime fun!

June 17, 2004

LOSS

GOODBYE

Lifted on the wings of a dove,
To mansions filled with God's immense love.
No more sadness
No more pain
Only joy and happiness
'Tis truly Heaven's gain.
Into Thy Hands I commit you.
God's promises hold true.

February 21,1998,
A poem written about my mother's death

I RELEASE YOU

Dear Ann,

> I now give you back to your Heavenly Father
> In whom you had faith and to whom you belong.
> Your days of earthly suffering and weariness are over.
> Your faith, which sustained you while here on earth,
> Now carries you to your eternal home —
> No more pain, suffering or weariness.
> You are a new creature in Christ!
> As you depart from your friends and loved ones,
> I release you safely into the arms of Jesus
> Now and forevermore.

September 7, 1998

LETTING GO

Letting Go – cleaning the closets of my life,
Throwing out years' worth of garbage,
Which weighs me down with extra baggage.

Letting Go – releasing that which has a hold on me,
Ridding self of once seemingly meaningful possessions,
Also feelings of – deep hurt, anger and confusion.

Letting Go – leaving behind the things that bind and hamper me,
Things that prevent me from progressing
And continuously cause stumbles and falls.

Letting Go – lightening the load,
Leaving behind tons of baggage,
No longer weighed down by the burdens of life .

Letting Go – a freeing experience!

April 7, 2000

This is the first poem I wrote after November 18, 1999. This
poem is written to commemorate a "burning ceremony" held on
April 13, 2000, by Pastor David Morgan and myself to "burn"
documents that I had shared with a prior counselor — to let go of
the memory-centered scrapbook, which was weighing me down.

LETTING YOU GO

Letting you go is a frightening process — for us both . . .
We're both sailing into unchartered territory.
Yet,
God has us in His palm, leading each of us by the hand.

For you . . .
Your ninety-year-old body, which has begun to give out,
will soon find rest.
There will be no more weariness, pain or fear.
You will once again be with your beloved Mary . . .

For me . . .
I will go on and I will be okay.
God has surrounded me with
a choice, first-class support system —
A good mix of professionals,
as well as "old" and new friends.
These will help see me through the rough times.

I release you now into God's hands,
to allow you to sail off into the horizon.

September 2, 2001

FROM ASHES TO ASHES

From ashes to ashes
And dust to dust
I now return you to . . .
That from which you were created,
As well as to the One who created you —
The Lord our God

June 14, 2002

FOR TOMMY

I Miss You

Tommy, I miss you so
It is so hard for me, to let you go.
Your spirit is all around me;
Wherever the wind doth blow.

You departed this earth all too fast;
We had a friendship made to last.
Our time together quickly passed.

I know you're in a better place
For, now you can see Jesus' face
And, in His arms you are safe.

November 9, 2005

YOU WILL BE MISSED

Oh, furry friend—you will be missed.
Your wet kisses
And your warm body next to mine—will be missed.
Your unassuming acceptance
And your snuggles under the covers—will be missed.
Your excitement at going for walks and chasing tennis balls
And your "dinnertime dance"—will be missed.
Oh, black and white furry friend—you will be missed.
Zach—you will be missed.

May 25, 2006

ZACH

DEPRESSION

OVERWHELMED BY LIFE

Perceiving the world in the wrong ways: Dysfunction

Vulnerable instead of protected
Conformity rather than a free spirit
Fear instead of confidence
Distrust rather than trust
Helplessness instead of capability
Defeated rather than successful
Nervous instead of calm
Shy rather than outgoing
Rejected instead of loved
Angry rather than happy
Frustrated instead of challenged
Hurt rather than content
Turmoil instead of tranquility
Despair rather than certainty
Trapped instead of free
Unloved rather than accepted
Anxious instead of peaceful

Overwhelmed by life
But determined to overcome

July 24, 1999

WHAT DO I DO?

Dear God,
    What do I do when I'm about to crack?
    What do I do when all I seem to do is cry?
    What do I do when I'm ready to scream?
    What do I do when I want out?
    What do I do when my psychiatrist throws me out?
    What do I do when I can't seem to talk?
    What do I do when I can't communicate except
        with a bunch of silly words on a piece of paper?
    What do I do when I become violent with myself?
    What do I do when I feel like killing myself-
        if only I had the courage?
    What do I do when there's no one to listen?
    What do I do when there's no place left to turn?
    What can I do?

February 25, 1977

BOUND

Bound by chains
Bound by chains of fear
Bound by chains of frustration
Bound by chains of anxiety
Bound by chains of . . .
Tied in knots
Tense through and through
Lord, set me free.

September 12, 1978

ALL STIRRED UP

Confusion,
Questions,
Fear,
Grief,
Sadness,
Happiness,
Joy,
Wonderment and awe
All stirred up within,
Like a pressure cooker about to boil over,
Like a geyser about to spew.
I make no apologies for asking for what I need
For I know that I'm worthy in God's eyes.

March 31, 1998

PAIN

Pain – It builds and builds and builds.
A race against time
Until it reaches a crescendo and explodes.
The explosion brings with it fallout . . .
Torrents of tears . . .
Creating a raging sea of emotion
Sweeping over me in waves,
Gradually becoming calmer and calmer and calmer.

March 10, 1999

DEPRESSION – ONE

Locked within depression's grip,
Feeling as if . . .
I've been punched with an ironclad fist,
Out of control,
Spiraling downward,
Upset stomach,
Pounding head,
Irregular breathing,
Agitated,
Pacing the room,
Itching,
Depression.

When will it loosen its grip upon me?

April 11, 1999

DEPRESSION – TWO

Depression takes hold of my life,
Spreading like wildfire,
Permeating all areas of life.
Thinking becomes clouded
Like wandering in a sea of fog.
Feelings are shut down
Like a frozen block of ice.
Joy is elusive
Like a butterfly flying to and fro.
The road up is a long one.
The battle has only just begun.

April 19, 1999

DEPRESSION – THREE

Caught in the web of depression
Like a spider's captured prey,
Having the wind knocked out of me
Like a sailboat without its power.
Difficulty staying afloat
Like a sinking ship at sea,
Floundering back and forth
Like a fish out of water.

Will I sink or will I swim?

April 21, 1999

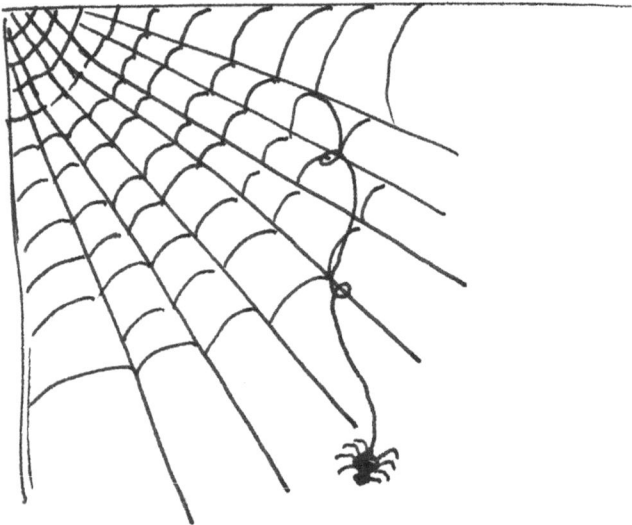

DEPRESSION – FOUR

Paralyzed,
Unable to move forward,
Stuck in a vacuum,
Suspended in time and space.
Standing on the outside,
An observer,
Watching the parade of life go by.

May 2, 1999

HURT

Many feelings:
Mixed up and confused — deep within.
Hurt and pain,
Swirling — rising to the top.
Tears slowly seeping out, around the edges.
Like a geyser — ready to errupt,
A pressure cooker — about to spew,
A time-bomb — ready to explode.
Fallout, from the explosion — strewn all about.
Feelings everywhere
Affecting all of life.

October 16, 1999

SPIRALING DOWNWARD

Snowflakes spiraling down to the ground,
I, too, begin spiraling downward,
Trapped inside by cold, icy weather.
Feelings trapped within—desperately wanting out,
Snow continually falling—the depths quickly rising.
Anxiety mounting,
Panic.
Waiting for the meltdown . . .
Sunshine once again,
Finally set free.

November 18, 1999

OUT OF CONTROL

Life spins out of control
Like the engines on a jet plane.
At first slowly, then faster and ever faster,
My mind is racing and spinning.
Like playground merry-go-rounds of old,
No end in sight.
Feelings of chaos—depression takes hold.

May 27, 2001

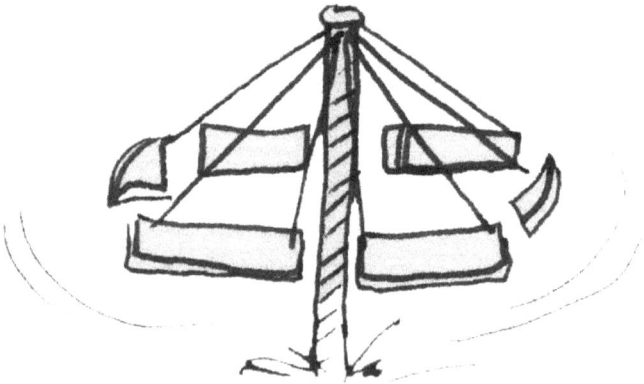

SINKING

Depression usurps,
Quickly sinking like quicksand,
Being pulled in and sucked under, as if in a vaccum.
Trapped in a pit of despair,
Frantically trying to get out,
Depression engulfs.

May 27, 2001

LOST

Lost in a foreign land,
Wandering to and fro,
Not knowing which way to go.

Veiled in the darkness of grief,
As in a shroud of fog,
Cobwebs at every turn.

The path is like a maze,
Doubling back at every turn,
A never-ending journey.

April 2007

WHERE ARE YOU?

God, where are you?
I can't seem to find you
Amid the mess my life is in,
Yet I know You are out there
   In the sky,
   The stars,
   The trees,
   The sea,
Also in Your love, surrounding me
By family, friends and professionals
Who support and uplift me
When I'm having difficulty walking.

Oh, Lord,
I ask not only for your patience
But also for the patience of those surrounding me
As I make an effort to pull myself together
And become whole, once again.

                – Amen

          July 2, 2009

SUPPORT

GROWING PAINS

My heart's aflutter,
Stirred up, awakened.
Excitement,
A sense of wonderment and awe,

Confusion.
Questions abound,
Emotions running wild
Like a roller coaster ride.

Pain,
Overwhelmed with grief and sadness,
Faced with many losses.

There's healing amid Your chosen ones,

Tempered,
Soothed like a balm,
Held in God's palm,
Calmed by God's great love.

March 16, 1998

REFOCUSED

Refocused,
New strength from above,
Refreshed,
Ready to continue the climb toward God's love,
Reaching for new heights,
Ascending like a dove.

Mach 16, 1998

I AM HELD

I am held in the palm of His Hand.
I am uplifted by those who walk on either side of me,
    as well as those who encircle me.
I am strengthened by the One who lives within me.
I am empowered by the One who created me.

June 3, 1998

CONNECTEDNESS

One human soul connected to another
Like gears interlocking, meshing with one another,
Working smoothly.
A sense of completeness
Like a dolphin dance, molded to one another,
Responding to one another's ups and downs,
Beauty at its best,
A sense of wholeness,
Love in in its purest form.
God's Love.

September 18, 1998

UNDERSTANDING

The understanding of another,
Sensitivity to another's unspoken needs,
The key which unlocks the door to the recesses of the soul.
The understanding of another,
Cleansing, liberating and healing.

January 8,1999

TEACHER

A teacher gently nudges to motivate us.
A teacher guides us to success.
A teacher takes the time to counsel
  with words of wisdom and of truth.
A good teacher excites and makes us want to learn.
One teacher comes in the form of the Holy Spirit,
The Comforter and Teacher.

June 1, 1999

I AM HELD – TWO

I am lifted up,
I am connected
By God's Spirit
And by Love.
I am held tightly.
I am wrapped . . .
I am encompassed in the palm of
God's Hand.

July 1, 2001

THIS HOUSE IS BLESSED

This house is blessed.
It's halls are hallowed.
Its floors are worn by family and friends.
Its rooms are filled with laughter, warmth and love.
May the Lord's peace be imparted —
To all who enter here.
Amen

August 5, 2002

Note: This poem is written about Anne and David Morgan's home
where I have stayed on many occasions, whether it
be petsitting and/or "Grandma" sitting.

EVER CHANGING

Some days bring frustration
While others bring happiness.
Just as the seasons change,
I, too, change.
Some days find me slipping into my old ways of immaturity
While others find tremendous growth, sprouting new wings.
Still others find me without a care, living freely.
Every day is ever changing
As I'm emerging into a new self-awareness.

August 5,1979

THANK YOU FOR BEING THERE

In my losses and in my gains,
In my sadness and in my grief,
In my joys and in my happiness,
Thank You for being there.

In life's celebrations
And the rituals that accompany them,
In my failures and in my successes,
In my struggle to make life work,
Thank You for being there.

Thank You for being there — in all of life.

October 25, 2005

Dedicated to
Rev. David Morgan,
my pastor, counselor, mentor and friend

MY SISTER

My sister,
A friend
With whom
I can laugh,
Hug,
Cry,
Giggle
And share secrets.

My sister,
A friend
Who shares my background and upbringing,
Who knows me like no other.

My sister,
A friend
With whom
I shop,
Cook and eat
And travel.

My sister,
A friend
Whom I can't do without.

August 14, 2008

TRUE BLUE FRIENDS

True blue friends are loyal,
Are always there,
And a breath of fresh air.
True blue friends
Willingly lend an ear
To hear.
True blue friends
Are dear to the heart
From the start.
True blue friends
Hold one another together
And make the world better.
True blue friends
Inspire laughter
And are there
For happily ever after.
True blue friends
Will walk with you along the way
And are here to stay!

April 17, 2012

HOPE

WELLSPRINGS

Wellsprings,
Wellsprings of life
Overflow from deep within.
Within the depths of my soul,
I can no longer contain them.
I must express my feelings of
love,
joy,
gratitude,
happiness,
excitement,
wonderment and
awe.

I must express my feelings of
confusion,
pain,
guilt,
sadness,
fear,
depression and
anxiety too.

Expression of all these feelings
Cleanse, heal and lead to
Wellsprings of life —
New Life!

May 13,1998

SEWING/SOWING

In and out, in and out, in and out
God has a pattern, a master design for my life.
He sows seeds of want—
Hungering, thirsting,
I search for His truths
So that I might apply them in my life.
In and out, in and out, in and out
God continues to sow,
Preparing the soil of my heart.
The Holy Spirit draws me
So that I might receive and act upon His truth.
In and out, in and out, in and out
His Word pierces my heart like a dart.

May 25, 1998

GOD'S LOVE

God's love is made real this Christmas night
Through God's son—incarnate
Through, a touch, a word, a hug,
Through a family of believers,
Through the miracle of life,
God's love is made real.

December 25, 1998

In praise and thanksgiving for my New Hope "family"
and especially for David and his ministry and his life—
he is still here among us!

HEAL ME

Heal me,
Wash me,
Cleanse me,
Purify my heart.
Take the things that keep me apart.
Take from me my sin.
Set me free within.
Mold me and make me new again.

April 3, 1999

HOLY LORD

Holy Lord,
I come before you,
Kneeling in your presence,
Asking for your forgiveness
For the transgressions I have committed against others.

Holy Lord,
Kneeling in your presence,
I bow my head before you—in prayerful meditation.

Holy Lord,
I arise with arms outstretched,
Standing in awe before you.
Bathed in the sunlight of your love,
I now accept your forgiveness and your grace.

March 15, 2004

HIS STEADFAST LOVE

Lost in a vast maze
Of time and space,
God's strength and power
Bids us come . . .

Come to a holy place,
A place where peace, strength and power are found.

An Altar, where God's steadfast love abounds
So, that we may dwell therein forever.

March 29, 2004

RENEWED

Lord, I stand before you now,
Arms outstretched,
Bursting forth
As is all of life
In the springtime of the year.

Trees budding
Flowers blooming
Bees buzzing
Plants sprouting
And butterflies emerging from cocoons.
It's a renewal and rebirth of life.

April 4, 2004

THANK YOU, LORD, FOR YOUR GREAT LOVE

Thank You, Lord, for your great love,
a love that encompasses me
and holds me close to your breast,
a love that knows my every need
even before it is spoken,
a love that knows my every thought
and understands me at my core,
a love that is there in spite of myself,
a love that accepts me
with my imperfections
a love thatgently invites me to grow;
yet, rremains when I don't succeed
thank-you, Lord, for your great love,
a love that is never ending.

June 7, 2004

DO NOT LOOK BACK

Do not look back,
Only look forward.
Look forward to
The possibilities,
The possibilities of
New friends,
New adventures,
New ideas,
New opportunities of every kind.
"Seize the day."
Live one day at a time.

August 28, 2008

I AM

I am Abby

I am a woman.
I am powerful.
I am an individual with a voice.

I am a writer,
A poet,
A singer,
Giving meaning to
The words at the depth of my soul.

I am a helper,
An aide to
Children,
The elderly,
And all who are in need of assistance.

I am creative.
I am a scrapbooker,
A designer (collages).
I am a creator,
Creating community with those surrounding me.

August 28, 2008

THIS BOAT

This boat,
This vessel
Is sturdy.
This boat will
Keep me afloat
When
With certainty
The storms come.
This boat is
Weathered and worn,
Yet
This boat keeps me afloat.

May 23, 2010

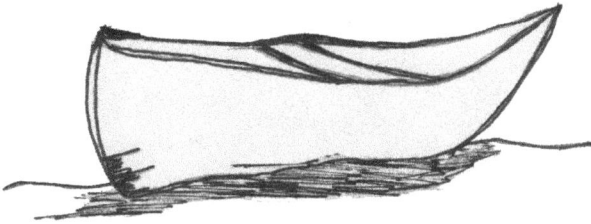

73

STURDY OLD OAK

Time worn and battered
By storms through the years,
Yet its branches
Reach out to embrace,
Offering shelter from the sun.

June 6, 2010

I AM HELD – THREE

In the midst of chaos and turmoil
And my life that has fallen apart,
I am held.

No need to pretend.
I am met where I'm at—
At my point of need.
And then,
God dealt with the situation at hand.
 I am held.

When I can't walk
"There is only one set of footprints"[1]
I am carried,
I am held.

There is grace in every moment
The grace of
God's great Love,
Free for the asking.
I am lifted,
Lifted high.
 In God's great Love
 I am held

September 11, 2008

---

1 "Footprints in the Sand," Multiple authors.

ACKNOWLEDGMENTS

I thank the following for their input, inspiration and guidance: Mrs. Ostborg, Mrs. Penny Weaver, Dr. Don W. King, Rev. David Morgan, Nancy Zimmerman, Eunice Sandra Morse and Rita Mudry.

I thank Becky LedBetter for her illustrations and Nancy B. Webster for her photography. I thank Nancy Dillingham for her skilled poetry proof reading, which helped make this book better.

Finally, I thank Grateful Steps and Micki Cabaniss Eutsler for her love and support throughout the process and without whom this book would not be possible.

www.ingramcontent.com/pod-product-compliance
Lightning Source LLC
Chambersburg PA
CBHW041929040426
42445CB00018B/1945